IBRAHIM TRAORE

The Revolutionary Leader Who
Reshaped Burkina Faso's Political
Landscape And Inspired A New Era
Of Pan-Africanism

Simon C. Batson

All rights reserved. No part of this publication may be reproduced, distributed, or transmitted in any form or by any means, including photocopying, recording, or other electronic or mechanical method, without the prior written permission of the publisher, except in the case of brief quotations embodied in critical reviews and certain other noncommercial uses permitted by the copyright law.

Copyright © **Simon C. Batson**, 2025.

TABLE OF CONTENT

INTRODUCTION

CHAPTER 1: HUMBLE BEGINNINGS AND MILITARY ASPIRATIONS
Traoré's Childhood, Education, And Early Influences
His Decision To Join The Military And Rise Through The Ranks
Lessons Learned From Burkina Faso's Past Leaders, Especially Thomas Sankara

CHAPTER 2: A NATION IN CRISIS – THE PATH TO THE COUP
Growing Instability In Burkina Faso
Public Frustration With Previous Leadership
The Conditions That Led Traoré's Military Intervention

CHAPTER 3: THE 2022 COUP – A TURNING POINT
The Events Leading Up To The Coup
Important Figures And The Reasons For The Military Coup
The Immediate Reaction From The Burkinabé People And The International Community

CHAPTER 4: RECLAIMING NATIONAL SOVEREIGNTY

Breaking Away From Neocolonial Influence
Traoré's Bold Stance Against French Military Presence
Realigning Burkina Faso's International Partnerships

CHAPTER 5: THE SECURITY DILEMMA – FIGHTING FOR STABILITY
Strategies To Combat Terrorism And Insurgency
Strengthening The military And local defense initiatives
Regional Security Alliances With Mali And Niger

CHAPTER 6: THE PAN-AFRICAN DREAM – A UNITED AFRICA
Traoré's Vision For African Economic And Political Independence
Strengthening Ties With Revolutionary Leaders Across The Continent
Advocating For Self-Reliance And Intra-African Cooperation

CHAPTER 7: CHALLENGES FROM WITHIN AND ABROAD
Opposition From Political Elites And Economic Struggles
Foreign Media Narratives, Diplomatic Difficulties, And Western sanctions
Internal Resistance And Governance Obstacles

CHAPTER 8: MOBILIZING THE YOUTH AND GRASSROOTS MOVEMENTS
The Role Of Young People In Burkina Faso's Revolution

Economic And Educational Measures To Empower The Next Generation
Building A Sustainable Model Of Leadership For The Future

CHAPTER 9: THE LEGACY OF A REVOLUTIONARY LEADER
Ibrahim Traoré's Impact On Burkina Faso And Africa's Future
Lessons From His Leadership And The Resurgence Of Pan-Africanism
The Ongoing Transformation And What Lies Ahead

CONCLUSION

INTRODUCTION

Throughout history, certain individuals have emerged as transformative forces, reshaping the destiny of their nations and leaving an indelible mark on the course of global events. Ibrahim Traoré, the young and enigmatic leader of Burkina Faso, is one such figure. His sudden rise to power in 2022 sent shockwaves across Africa and beyond, as he swiftly dismantled the status quo and charted a bold new path for his country. In an era of political uncertainty, economic dependency, and ongoing security threats, Traoré's leadership represents a dramatic shift toward sovereignty, self-reliance, and a renewed Pan-African vision.

Burkina Faso, a landlocked West African nation with a rich but turbulent history, has long been a battleground for competing interests both internal and external. From the legacy of its revolutionary hero, Thomas Sankara, to the challenges of modern-day insurgencies and political instability, the country has struggled to assert its independence from the shadows of neocolonial influence. By the time Traoré emerged as a leader, the Burkinabé people were yearning for change. Their patience with ineffective governance had worn thin, and the security crisis posed by extremist groups had reached catastrophic levels. It was in this context that Captain Ibrahim Traoré, a young but determined military officer, stepped forward to assume the mantle of leadership.

The political and security landscape of Burkina Faso prior to Traoré's rise was dire. The country, like many of its Sahelian neighbors, was plagued by a growing insurgency that had displaced millions and claimed thousands of lives. Jihadist groups, emboldened by weak governance and porous borders, controlled vast swaths of territory, leaving rural populations vulnerable to terror and lawlessness. Previous administrations, despite military assistance from Western powers such as France, failed to curb the violence, and trust in government institutions eroded rapidly. Against this backdrop, frustration mounted among soldiers on the frontlines who bore the brunt of the failed counterterrorism strategies. Many felt abandoned by their superiors and disillusioned with a government that seemed more accountable to foreign interests than to its own people. It was this frustration that set the stage for the September 30, 2022, coup, which saw Traoré depose Lieutenant Colonel Paul-Henri Sandaogo Damibawho himself had seized power just months earlier. With the backing of young officers and widespread public support, Traoré quickly established himself as the face of a new movement: one that sought to restore national dignity and security through radical, uncompromising action.

Unlike many of his predecessors, Ibrahim Traoré's leadership style has been unapologetically bold. He has distanced himself from the influence of France, Burkina Faso's former colonial ruler, and has openly criticized the continued presence of Western military forces in the region. His decision to expel French troops and seek alternative security partnerships with Russia and other non-Western allies has signaled a major geopolitical shift, one that has inspired other African nations to reconsider their own foreign alliances. This move, while controversial, was met with widespread support from Burkinabé citizens who had grown weary of perceived Western exploitation and ineffective foreign interventions. It also positioned Traoré as a key figure in the broader Pan-African movement, one that advocates for economic independence, military self-sufficiency, and stronger regional alliances free from external manipulation.

But leading a revolution is never without challenges. Internally, Traoré faces resistance from political elites, economic uncertainties, and the continued threat of terrorism. Internationally, he has drawn both admiration and condemnation, with Western governments wary of his growing ties with alternative global powers. Yet, despite the odds, he has remained steadfast in his mission to redefine Burkina Faso's future on its own terms. His leadership has ignited a newfound sense of hope, particularly among the country's youth, who see in him the possibility of a Burkina Faso that is not merely a pawn in global politics but a sovereign nation charting its own destiny.

The rise of Ibrahim Traoré is more than just the story of a military officer who took power, it is the story of a people reclaiming their agency. It is the resurgence of a revolutionary spirit that has long been embedded in Burkina Faso's history, from the era of Thomas Sankara to the present day. His leadership represents a crucial turning point, not only for his country but for Africa as a whole, as it grapples with questions of self-determination, governance, and economic independence. This book explores into the journey of a man who has defied expectations, reshaped Burkina Faso's political landscape, and reignited the flames of Pan-Africanism in a way that may very well change the continent's future.

CHAPTER 1: HUMBLE BEGINNINGS AND MILITARY ASPIRATIONS

Traoré's Childhood, Education, And Early Influences

In Burkina Faso, a historically significant but politically unstable nation, Ibrahim Traoré was born into a humble family. The reality of a country trying to define itself in the face of economic hardship and security concerns influenced his formative years. He grew up seeing the everyday hardships of common Burkinabé folks in an atmosphere where survival often relied on resiliency. He showed a keen sense of curiosity and tenacity at an early age, traits that would later characterize his leadership.

An important factor in forming Traoré's perspective was his education. He was renowned for his academic interest and discipline when he was a student. He completed his early schooling in Burkina Faso, where he excelled in topics that called for problem-solving and critical thinking. He was profoundly influenced by the political history of the nation, particularly by Thomas Sankara's revolutionary ideas. Known as Africa's "Che Guevara," Sankara promoted independence, anti-corruption, and opposition to outside interference. Growing up in a generation that respected Sankara's vision but saw its promises unmet because succeeding administrations failed to maintain his ideals, Traoré found great resonance in his legacy.

He became quite interested in national security and military strategy as his studies went on. Because of this enthusiasm, he enrolled in the military school in Burkina Faso, where he received intense training. He developed a feeling of responsibility, self-control, and leadership at the school. In addition to learning the technical aspects of combat, he also learnt the value of strategy, fortitude, and flexibility in times of crisis. He became aware of Burkina Faso's security issues during his military service, especially the increasing danger of insurgency in the Sahel.

He saw firsthand the shortcomings of government strategies in combating terrorism and safeguarding civilians during his early deployments, which put him on the frontlines. He saw how the military was undermined by corruption, how troops lacked sufficient supplies, and how foreign interference often put interests outside of the country's borders ahead of its stability. His discontent with the current leadership grew as a result of these encounters. As he realized that the nation needed a new kind of government, he started to build close relationships with other troops who felt the same discontent.

Traoré was greatly impacted by Pan-Africanism and the larger fight for African sovereignty in addition to his military training. He studied a great deal about African leaders who battled for freedom and opposed colonialism. His conviction that Burkina Faso and Africa required leaders who put their country's interests ahead of those of other countries was strengthened by their hardships. His subsequent actions, especially his opposition to neocolonial influence and his advocacy for regional integration, were shaped by this intellectual basis.

Traoré had already formulated a vision for transformation by the time he advanced through the military levels. His early experiences, education, and upbringing molded him into a leader who valued deeds above words. He was driven by a desire to address the institutional shortcomings he had seen throughout his life, in contrast to those who sought power for their own benefit. He was ready for his eventual part in Burkina Faso's political change because of these early years.

His Decision To Join The Military And Rise Through The Ranks

Ibrahim Traoré's strong sense of responsibility and determination to defend his nation from the escalating dangers it faced motivated him to enlist in the military. He saw firsthand as a young man how Burkina Faso's security situation worsened year after year, with rural populations bearing the brunt of the expansion of extremist organizations. Many were dissatisfied by the government's incapacity to stop these dangers, particularly young Burkinabé who wanted to see their country become powerful and independent. Traoré saw the military as a way to serve and protect his people, not merely a way to pursue a career.

He enlisted at Burkina Faso's military school after finishing his formal education, where he received intense instruction in strategic planning, leadership, and combat tactics. Although the school was renowned for turning out well-behaved officers, it also made him aware of the inefficiencies and corruption that plagued the institution. Despite these difficulties, Traoré performed very well throughout his training and soon established himself as a committed and strategic commander. His ability to command respect from his peers and his keen intuition were noted by his superiors.

After graduating, he was sent to some of the most unstable areas of the nation, where armed groups regularly attacked security personnel and people. His fortitude and leadership were put to the test during these early missions. Traoré led his soldiers from the front, gaining their respect and faith in contrast to many commanders who stayed far away from the action. He saw firsthand the terrible effects of corruption on military operations, the dearth of appropriate equipment, and the central government's poor assistance. His determination to demand change was further bolstered by his difficulties.

As he advanced through the ranks, Traoré joined a new generation of commanders who began to doubt the nation's leadership. Since political elites were shielded from the fighting while troops were rushed into war without sufficient supplies, many in the military felt abandoned. He immediately gained notoriety for being frank in his support of a more capable and independent military. He was given leadership roles in important operations because of his capacity to motivate people and his strategic thinking.

He was instrumental in counterterrorism operations throughout his service, helping to retake regions that extremist organizations had taken over. His victories on the battlefield showed not just his tactical prowess but also his capacity to inspire and unify men under trying circumstances. Traoré felt Burkina Faso needed to build its own military capabilities, even if top government officials mostly depended on international aid. He became a recognized figure in the military as his influence grew, especially among younger commanders who shared his views on national security and sovereignty.

The level of discontent in the military has escalated by 2022. Lieutenant Colonel

Paul-Henri Sandaogo Damiba had assumed command earlier that year but had not implemented significant reforms, and soldiers were beginning to lose trust in his leadership. Traoré and his supporters saw a chance to change the country's direction as dissatisfaction increased. He had been prepared for this moment by his ascent through the ranks. He was now a leader prepared to act decisively, not merely a soldier.

Lessons Learned From Burkina Faso's Past Leaders, Especially Thomas Sankara

In addition to his combat experiences, Traoré's political outlook was influenced by the teachings of Burkina Faso's previous leaders, especially Thomas Sankara. From 1983 until his death in 1987, Sankara, sometimes referred to as the "African Che Guevara," governed Burkina Faso, leaving a legacy of radical self-reliance, anti-corruption measures, and Pan-African values. Traoré found in him an example of what genuine leadership ought to be, and his leadership style, dedication to the people, and rejection of neocolonial influence struck a deep chord with him.

Sankara's emphasis on national sovereignty was his most distinctive quality. According to him, Burkina Faso needs to break away from foreign economic dominance and establish its own manufacturing, agricultural, and military capacities. By encouraging local manufacturing and resource management, he sought to reduce reliance on outside sources and refused to be a puppet of Western powers. Growing up at a period when Burkina Faso was still strongly dependent on former colonial powers, Traoré saw the end of a revolutionary era with Sankara's killing. His initiatives were mostly abandoned by the governments that came after him, who instead relied on military assistance and foreign aid that did nothing to fortify the nation. This historical violation of Sankara's principles had a significant impact on Traoré's outlook on politics.

Traoré also learned from Sankara how important it is to put the needs of the people above those of the political class. In addition to lowering government wages and wasteful expenditure, Sankara is renowned for rejecting opulent perks and setting an example of self-discipline and simplicity. His people-centered administration placed a strong emphasis on women's rights, healthcare, and education. Traoré realized that genuine change could only occur under leadership that really served the interests of the people rather than the ruling class after seeing the corruption and self-serving character of many of the leaders who followed Sankara. His conviction that any revolution must be based on serving the country rather than pursuing personal goals was strengthened when he saw how successive rulers had amassed wealth while the average Burkinabé lived in poverty and insecurity.

Traoré also took note of the errors that ultimately brought Sankara to ruin. Sankara's alienation of influential elites, including his closest supporters, who eventually turned against him, was one of the main causes of his death. Sankara's leadership style sometimes lacked the political skill required to handle domestic resistance, despite his vision and bravery in opposing foreign authority. Recognizing this historical lesson, Traoré understood that he would need to win over important political and social sectors in addition to the military in order to maintain change. He understood that in order to avoid the blunders that had cost Sankara his life, revolutionary objectives needed to be supported by strategic partnerships.

Traoré researched the leadership of other African revolutionaries who opposed foreign rule, such as Kwame Nkrumah, Patrice Lumumba, and Muammar Gaddafi, in addition to Sankara. He used their hardships, triumphs, and eventual failures as a guide to help him negotiate the challenging terrain of African leadership. He was aware that achieving full independence would be difficult and that strong international interests would oppose any leader who tried to do it. But he also thought that Burkina Faso could not afford to continue to be mired in a cycle of poor governance and reliance.

Traoré had already digested these principles by the time he came to power. He was aware that regaining Burkina Faso's sovereignty was necessary and would not be granted to him. He was aware that actions, not just words, were required to gain the confidence of the populace. Most significantly, he was aware that leaders who attacked the international system without sufficient planning had already suffered the consequences, as history had shown. Equipped with these realizations, he embarked on a mission to rebuild Burkina Faso's future, resurrecting the revolutionary spirit of Sankara while avoiding the errors of the past.

CHAPTER 2: A NATION IN CRISIS – THE PATH TO THE COUP

Growing Instability In Burkina Faso

As Ibrahim Traoré advanced in the military, Burkina Faso was experiencing increasing instability. Political unpredictability, mass displacement, and deadly insurgencies have turned the hitherto tranquil country into a battlefield. The state of security had quickly deteriorated to the point that the government no longer controlled large areas of the nation. The Burkinabé people experienced a climate of discontent and anxiety as a result of this crisis, which was exacerbated by terrorist assaults, poor government, and international meddling. Traoré and his generation of warriors faced an increasingly difficult struggle to protect their motherland in this uncertain environment.

Internal flaws and external dangers were the main causes of Burkina Faso's instability. Using the Sahel region's open borders, poverty, and weakened state institutions, extremist organizations associated with al-Qaeda and the Islamic State have been expanding their activities there for years. These organizations took advantage of local concerns, especially in rural regions with little government presence. Residents fled for their lives, leaving whole towns abandoned, and the government found it difficult to provide even the most basic protection. In areas where the state had all but disappeared, armed groups established their own harsh authority, carried out atrocities, and destroyed infrastructure.

The inability of succeeding administrations to establish a successful response made the issue worse. The security forces of Burkina Faso continued to be ill-prepared and disorganized in spite of military assistance and collaborations with Western friends. Due to corruption in the military and administration, funds intended for counterterrorism operations were often mishandled or never made it to frontline troops. Resentment within the military was exacerbated by this inefficiency and lack of responsibility, as soldiers felt abandoned while against a more formidable foe.

The Burkinabé people lost trust in their leaders as the government's hold loosened. Nationwide protests broke out as people called for a more robust reaction to the escalating insecurity. Frustration evolved into demands for radical change, and protests centered on Ouagadougou, the capital. Even the military, which has traditionally been seen as the final line of defense, was losing credibility as a result of its many military failures, and the public no longer trusted their elected representatives to defend them.

President Roch Marc Christian Kaboré was overthrown in a military coup headed by Lieutenant Colonel Paul-Henri Sandaogo Damiba in January 2022 as a result of this growing dissatisfaction. Many people were originally optimistic about the coup because they thought a government dominated by the military would act decisively against the rebels. But the military and the populace were soon let down by Damiba's reign. Those who want a more autonomous strategy were further disillusioned by his administration's failure to fulfill its promises of restoring security and his prolonged dependence on French military assistance. Burkina Faso was on the brink of collapse by the middle of 2022, and the situation remained terrible.

Ibrahim Traoré became a leader who was prepared to take drastic measures to resolve the situation in this setting. He was regarded by many in the military as a leader who really sympathized with the plight of both troops and civilians. Traoré had been on the frontlines for years, unlike his predecessors who stayed far away from the reality on the ground. He had seen the price of poor leadership and felt that Burkina Faso could only be saved from total collapse by taking decisive, audacious action.

Dissatisfaction among the military reached a critical point by September 2022. Once-supporting soldiers turned against Damiba, accusing him of failure and ineptitude. On September 30, 2022, Traoré staged a second attempt to overthrow Damiba, with the increasing backing of his fellow military. Traoré was clear from the beginning that his administration would not accept foreign influence or weak policies, in contrast to past presidents who sought compromise. He pledged to restore security, restore confidence in the government, and recapture Burkina Faso's sovereignty.

His ascent to power signaled a sea change in the history of the nation. His leadership had emerged as a result of the years-long instability that had afflicted Burkina Faso. Making promises a reality and demonstrating that this time, change will really happen was an even bigger task.ll

Public Frustration With Previous Leadership

Public dissatisfaction with Burkina Faso's previous administration had escalated to an all-time high by the time Ibrahim Traoré assumed office in September 2022. The Burkinabé people had been watching for years while their officials did little to address the deteriorating security situation, which allowed extremist groups to take control of vast swaths of the nation. Although every succeeding administration has pledged reform, the country's issues have only gotten worse due to corruption, incapacity, and dependence on outside forces. The populace sought tangible action because they were fed up with meaningless words.

For years, the frustration had been growing. Burkina Faso's security situation dramatically worsened during President Roch Marc Christian Kaboré, who held office from 2015 to 2022. Islamist terrorist attacks became more frequent and more intense, uprooting whole villages and forcing almost two million people to flee. In many places, basic services crumbled, schools closed, and farmers left their land. Kaboré's administration found it difficult to react appropriately to the deteriorating circumstances. Intelligence activities were not well-coordinated, and soldiers were not well equipped. Public trust was further damaged when rumors of corruption in the military leadership emerged.

Kaboré was overthrown in January 2022 by a military coup headed by Lieutenant Colonel Paul-Henri Sandaogo Damiba. Many Burkinabé originally applauded the coup, hoping that military authority would offer a more forceful approach to combating terrorism. As a soldier himself, Damiba pledged to restore lost lands and give security first priority. But after a few months, it was evident that not much had changed. Despite having experience in counterterrorism, Damiba was unable to put effective plans into action, and Islamist assaults persisted. Even worse, despite widespread opposition to foreign involvement, he maintained tight connections with France and let French forces operate in Burkina Faso.

Damiba's tenure was seen by the Burkinabé populace, especially the younger generation, as a continuation of the same unsuccessful policies that had beset earlier administrations. Many thought that rather than assisting, French military intervention was escalating instability. People in West Africa were demanding full independence from former colonial countries as part of a rising trend of Pan-Africanism. This view generated growing resentment against Damiba's administration in Burkina Faso, which was seen as being too close to international interests. Demonstrators demanded a new approach to administration and an end to French interference as protests broke out.

Discontent with Damiba also increased inside the military. Poor logistics, a dearth of reinforcements, and leadership that seemed disconnected from the reality of the battle continued to plague soldiers on the frontlines. While top leaders stayed in the capital, oblivious to the horrors of combat, many lower-ranking commanders and foot troops believed they were being sent to fight without the necessary support. Captain Ibrahim Traoré, a young but well-respected commander who had established a reputation for his leadership and combat expertise, was one of several who raised concerns.

The issue had gotten out of hand by the end of September 2022. Under the leadership of Traoré, a group of troops determined that Damiba could no longer hold onto control. They staged a coup on September 30 and quickly ousted him from power. Many individuals supported the takeover, especially young people who saw Traoré as a leader who sympathized with their plight. In contrast to his predecessors, he had shown his battle skills and was straightforward, honest, and unyielding in his opposition to foreign influence and corruption.

In addition to overthrowing Damiba, Traoré's ascent was a reaction to years of mounting dissatisfaction with Burkina Faso's governance.

The populace was fed up with leaders that promised things but never followed through. They want security, autonomy, and action. They saw a new kind of leader in Traoréone who dared to oppose both foreign meddling and domestic corruption. Though his ascent was greeted with excitement, the true test was still to come: could he bring about the transformation that so many others had failed to?

The Conditions That Led Traoré's Military Intervention

A number of factors, including deteriorating security, ineffective governance, outside influence, and growing discontent within the military and the populace at large, contributed to Ibrahim Traoré's military involvement. With millions of people displaced, over 40% of the nation controlled by extremist groups, and an all-time low in public faith in the government, Burkina Faso was on the brink of collapse by September 2022. The conditions were ideal for another military intervention since successive administrations failed to solve these issues.

The worsening security situation was one of the most urgent problems. Attacks by Islamist extremists had not only persisted but had become worse in January 2022, even after a military coup installed Lieutenant Colonel Paul-Henri Sandaogo Damiba. Major highways were made hazardous, villages were invaded often, and inhabitants were slaughtered. Due to inadequate government backing, inadequate equipment, and bad logistics, the nation's already overburdened military forces found it difficult to react effectively. Frontline soldiers felt abandoned as they fought a more formidable foe with less supplies.

The government's dependence on foreign powers, especially France, became a significant source of tension at the same time. Many Burkinabé thought that French military aid was just serving to prolong instability for geopolitical and commercial reasons rather than providing genuine answers. The government of neighboring Mali has already driven out French soldiers and resorted to new security alliances, like with Russia's Wagner Group. Burkina Faso's calls for a more autonomous and self-sufficient approach to national security were stoked by this expanding regional trend away from Western military engagement.

The military quickly became dissatisfied with Damiba's leadership. Many of the military who had first backed his revolution came to see that he was carrying on the failing policies of the previous administration. Counterterrorism tactics were ineffectual, soldiers were still ill-prepared, and leadership corruption went unchecked. Every day, frontline soldiers put their lives in danger, while the central leadership in Ouagadougou seemed more and more disconnected from their plight.

The planned strikes by Islamist organizations that shut off major cities from supply, depriving thousands of people of food, medication, and other necessities, were one of the tipping moments. The most prominent instance was the humanitarian disaster caused by the siege of Djibo, a city in the north that had been encircled by militants for months. Anger among troops and citizens increased as a result of this inability to safeguard vital areas.

The spokesman of the disgruntled troops was Captain Ibrahim Traoré, who had become well-known among his colleagues for his leadership and combat expertise. Traoré had been directly engaged in frontline operations and had personal knowledge of the severity of the situation, unlike many higher ranked officers. He and other young commanders believed that in order for Burkina Faso to survive, its military strategy and government needed to be completely redesigned.

Military tensions reached a critical point by the end of September 2022. Under the leadership of Traoré, a group of troops determined that Damiba could no longer hold onto control. They charged him of incapacity, inability to defend the nation, and betrayal of the revolutionary principles that had supported his own coup.

They carried out a quick and forceful coup September 30, 2022, toppling Damiba and installing Traoré as Burkina Faso's new leader.

The populace, especially the young people, who had lost all trust in the previous administration, enthusiastically embraced the intervention. People in Ouagadougou and other cities staged large-scale protests in favor of Traoré, waving Russian and Burkinabé flags to express their desire for a change in political direction. For many individuals, this coup seemed like a necessary course correction, in contrast to earlier ones that were viewed with mistrust.

Traoré's involvement was a reaction to long-standing shortcomings that had placed the nation at risk of disintegration, not just another attempt to seize power. Widespread discontent with the leadership's inability to take strong action throughout the crisis led to his takeover. But now that he was in charge, he had an even bigger task: transforming military involvement into significant political and security changes that would bring peace back to Burkina Faso.

CHAPTER 3: THE 2022 COUP – A TURNING POINT

The Events Leading Up To The Coup

Increasing security lapses, mounting military discontent, and increasing public ire at Lieutenant Colonel Paul-Henri Sandaogo Damiba's administration all contributed to the events that culminated in the coup that installed Captain Ibrahim Traoré. As humanitarian circumstances deteriorated, faith in the governing government quickly eroded, and jihadists controlled vast swaths of the nation, Burkina Faso was on the verge of collapse by September 2022.

The siege of northern cities, especially the city of Djibo, by Islamist militants was one of the most significant turning moments. For months, militants had been able to prevent thousands of civilians from accessing food, medicine, and other necessities, putting them in danger of hunger. The administration was seen to be weak and incapable of securing its own area when the military failed to breach these blockades. Entire areas had been rendered lawless by such assaults, and jihadist organizations had established their own government there, frightening residents and uprooting a large number of people. A feeling of fear was heightened nationwide as news of massacres, kidnappings, and targeted killings proliferated.

The morale of the troops was at an all-time low. Frontline soldiers felt abandoned, left to battle highly armed militants with no help from central leadership, poor coordination, and insufficient supplies. From the moment Damiba came to power in January 2022, frustration had been mounting over poor leadership, corruption, and poor management. At first, a lot of troops thought that dramatic change would come from a government run by the military. But eight months later, Damiba had fallen short of his pledges, and his leadership was becoming more and more seen as ineffectual. Since Mali had previously driven out French soldiers and looked for other security alliances, many Burkinabé saw his decision to keep tight connections with France as a violation of national sovereignty.

Armed forces tensions escalated to a boiling point by mid-September. An array of junior officers, among them Captain Ibrahim Traoré, had been more vocal in their displeasure. In contrast to Damiba, who was mostly kept out of the front lines, Traoré had been in the thick of things and had seen firsthand the hardships of his comrades. Because of his leadership, discipline, and dedication to defending his nation, he had gained respect throughout the ranks. He was embraced by many in the military, who thought he might provide the capable leadership needed to change Burkina Faso's course.

On September 29, it became clear that a change in power was impending. Within the military, there were rumors of an internal uprising developing because some commanders intended to confront Damiba about how he handled the situation. There was a lot of shooting that night in Ouagadougou, especially near important government and military institutions. Soldiers loyal to Traoré seized key locations across the city and erected roadblocks.

By the early hours of September 30, the coup was well underway. The rebel forces successfully overthrew Damiba by capturing the presidential palace and the offices of the national television network. With other troops on his side, Traoré made the announcement that Damiba had been deposed on national television later that day. He justified the coup by pointing to the deteriorating security situation, poor governance, and the necessity for a new strategy for Burkina Faso's governance. The nation will now adopt a more autonomous posture, he said, with an emphasis on restoring sovereignty, bolstering the military, and prioritizing the needs of the populace.

Following the coup, huge groups of people celebrated the change in government in Ouagadougou and other towns in the hours and days that followed. In the eyes of many, Traoré was a real patriot who was prepared to act bravely and who understood the pain of the people. Signifying their desire for a fresh approach to national security and a departure from French control, protesters hoisted Russian and Burkinabé flags. When Damiba's last efforts to restore control failed, he fled to Togo and tried to negotiate a peaceful surrender.

The events leading up to the coup were the consequence of months, if not years, of growing instability, poor leadership, and military dissatisfaction rather than a single incident. Taking power was not about pursuing personal goals for Traoré; rather, it was about responding to the demands of troops and residents who had lost all trust in their leaders. The objective now was clear: provide Burkina Faso with the security, sovereignty, and stability that it sorely needed. He was carrying the burden of leadership.

Important Figures And The Reasons For The Military Coup

The military coup that installed Captain Ibrahim Traoré was the product of a concerted effort by a number of officers and troops who had become disenchanted with Lieutenant Colonel Paul-Henri Sandaogo Damiba's leadership. A mix of patriotic aspirations, wartime disappointments, and the pressing need to bring stability back to a nation that was quickly falling into the hands of rebels drove these important characters.

Traoré was the youthful, combat-experienced commander at the center of the coup, much respected by his colleagues for his leadership on the battlefield. Traoré, in contrast to many top commanders who stayed in the capital, had personally seen the hardships of demoralized and ill-equipped soldiers against a merciless foe. Because of his firsthand experience in war, he was an easy candidate for support from other troops, especially when military dissatisfaction increased. His discipline, command of loyalty, and military experience were vital in bringing those who wanted change together.

Traoré was joined by a handful of troops and mid-level commanders that made up the nucleus of the coup. Due to faulty strategic choices made by high leadership, many of these people had lost companions while serving on the front lines. They believed that a government that seemed to be disconnected from the reality of war had deceived them by leaving soldiers vulnerable to ongoing assaults without sufficient supplies, intelligence assistance, or reinforcements. They were driven by a clear desire for a leader who would value military performance above political scheming and who would recognize the sacrifices they had made.

Damiba was accused of siding with France, which was one of the primary reasons that drove the coup. The military's prolonged reliance on French military support, according to many, was prolonging instability rather than aiding in the battle against terrorism. An organizing principle for the coup plotters was the conviction that France's intervention suited its own geopolitical objectives rather than Burkina Faso's security requirements. They believed that Damiba's unwillingness to consider other security alliances, such collaboration with Russia, as is the case in neighboring Mali, was an indication of weakness and submission to outside pressure.

The escalating humanitarian situation across the nation was another significant contributing cause to the coup. By September 2022, jihadist organizations had taken over almost half of Burkina Faso, and major towns like Djibo had been besieged for months. Many people suffered and were depressed as a result of the government's incapacity to supply basic requirements and safeguard these places. After seeing the destruction inflicted upon residents, soldiers assigned to protect these areas were enraged at the government's lack of urgency. Their choice to act against Damiba gained moral weight as a result of this escalating humanitarian crisis.

The internal conflict among the military was the coup's last catalyst. Damiba had lost the trust of many of his commanders, especially those who had first backed his coup against President Roch Marc Christian Kaboré in January. Over the course of the months, it became clear that Damiba's leadership was identical to that of his predecessor. His pledges to regain lost territory and restore security were never kept. A radical shift was evidently required due to the troops' disappointment and mounting pressure from an impatient public.

With widespread backing from troops who felt Burkina Faso needed a new path, the September 30, 2022, coup was not an act of impromptu but rather a well-planned military action. Their activities were driven by a strong sense of duty, resentment at ineffective leadership, and a desire to take charge of their country's future. Despite being the public face of the coup, Traoré had the support of a large group of officers and soldiers who believed that this was their last opportunity to bring Burkina Faso back to peace and independence.

The Immediate Reaction From The Burkinabé People And The International Community

The international community's cautious condemnation of Ibrahim Traoré's takeover was sharply contrasted with the Burkinabé people's enthusiastic support. Most people in Burkina Faso hailed the coup, especially the young people, military, and rural residents who had been the most harmed by the previous administration. On the other hand, expecting further instability, international countries and regional organizations voiced their grave concerns about yet another military coup in West Africa.

The ouster of Damiba was swiftly celebrated by joyous crowds in the streets of Ouagadougou and other major towns. His administration was seen by many as carrying on the failing leadership that had caused the nation to descend into anarchy. In the hopes that his leadership would bring a more forceful approach to combating insecurity and regaining national sovereignty, protesters shouted for Traoré. Similar to what had happened in neighboring Mali, some protesters hoisted Russian and Burkinabé flags, indicating a desire for a break from French dominance. A rising Pan-African mood that called for a break from neocolonial connections and the pursuit of independent military solutions was mirrored in the demands for new alliances.

The storming of the French embassy in Ouagadougou was one of the most notable instances of the public's response. There were rumors that France was helping Damiba plan a counteroffensive and hiding him. This prospect infuriated demonstrators, who gathered outside the embassy and called for France to withdraw entirely from Burkina Faso. In Bobo-Dioulasso, where the French cultural institution was also targeted, similar protests broke out. These accusations strengthened preexisting anti-French sentiment and strengthened popular support for Traoré's leadership, even though they were never formally verified.

Traoré's coup, however, was widely accepted within the military. Many troops saw the leadership transition as an essential step toward improved military support and strategy, particularly those who were stationed in high-conflict zones. Traoré was viewed as one of them, someone who had gone through the same hardships and was dedicated to genuine change, in contrast to Damiba, who had cut himself off from frontline soldiers. This internal military backing helped secure a seamless transition and averted any substantial counter-coup efforts.

On the other hand, the international community responded with skepticism and concern. The coup was swiftly denounced by the Economic Community of West African States (ECOWAS), which also voiced concern about the growing number of military takeovers in the area and demanded a restoration to civilian governance. Similar worries were expressed by the African Union, which cautioned that frequent coups might destabilize West Africa and threaten democratic administration. Although it was uncertain how much of an impact their remarks would have on the incoming leadership, both groups asked Traoré to uphold prior commitments for a transition to civilian government.

A more cautious approach was adopted by France, which was already losing support in the area. French authorities acknowledged the growing anti-French sentiment in Burkina Faso and chose to abstain from taking immediate action while formally renouncing the coup. The harm had already been done, and public opinion had firmly shifted against France's presence in the nation, even if the French authorities denied any role in hosting Damiba.

Concern about Burkina Faso's instability was voiced in declarations by other international powers, such as the US and the EU. But they mostly stayed polite in their comments, emphasizing appeals for stability over immediate action. In contrast, Russia used a more opportunistic approach. Pro-Russian voices across Africa applauded Traoré's ascent, despite the coup's initial lack of official recognition. They saw it as a further step in lessening Western dominance in the Sahel.

The Burkinabé people themselves had the most significant reaction, notwithstanding the worldwide censure. Deep discontent with previous leadership and a strong yearning for change were expressed in the broad support for Traoré. The coup's immediate aftermath marked a sea change in Burkina Faso's political course, one that would later reshape its foreign policy, military strategy, and sense of national identity.

CHAPTER 4: RECLAIMING NATIONAL SOVEREIGNTY

Breaking Away From Neocolonial Influence

Ibrahim Traoré's ascent to power and the response to his coup were largely driven by his desire to break free from neocolonial control. A yearning for sovereignty and independence from foreign rule had driven the general dissatisfaction among Burkinabé's populace, especially the young and soldiers, to a breaking point. For years, this feeling had been growing since it was believed that Burkina Faso's previous leadership had prioritized their tight ties with former colonial powers, especially France, above the country's actual security and progress.

For a large number of Burkinabé, the association with France represented the continuation of neocolonialism. Like many other African countries, Burkina Faso had to contend with the substantial influence of its former colonizer, especially in military affairs, even after obtaining independence in 1960. France has soldiers in Burkina Faso and other parts of the Sahel under the pretense of counterterrorism. However, this presence seemed more like a kind of control than a cooperation to many troops and townspeople. An inept approach to dealing with the escalating Islamist insurgency and a general dissatisfaction with Western meddling in African politics and security affairs were often linked to the French soldiers' prolonged deployment.

Burkina Faso was hardly the only country to experience this rising discontent with France.

The military administration in Mali, in particular, has started to disassociate itself from French influence by driving out French troops and looking for other options, such collaborating with Russia's Wagner Group. As these changes in foreign policy gathered momentum in the area, the Burkinabé people, especially the younger generation, started to see Traoré's revolution as a chance to follow suit and break free from France's swaying influence.

A prominent manifestation of the aspiration for independence was the public's response to the coup. The Russian and Burkinabé flags flown by crowds in Ouagadougou represented a drive for new alliances and a rejection of French rule. As they saw Traoré's military intervention as the start of a new age free from the restrictions of past colonial powers, protesters voiced their support for it. It was evident from the chanting and flag-waving throughout the demonstrations that many Burkinabé anticipated the coup would be the beginning of a drastic change in the nation's ties with other countries, particularly France.

Burkina Faso promptly showed that it wanted to pursue a foreign policy independent of the West under Traoré's leadership. Although it was unknown what his future ties would entail, the new regime's rhetoric stressed the need of separating from Western influence. The significance of national sovereignty and autonomy was emphasized in Traoré's statement after the coup, in which he stated his commitment to reconstructing the country and addressing the security problem. A populace weary of depending on military assistance and foreign aid that had failed to produce results found resonance in his statements.

Additionally, the military junta said that it would look into forming new military and diplomatic alliances, maybe with nations like Russia that had already established themselves as powerful players in the area. Burkina Faso's departure from France was presented as an attempt to reaffirm its independence and forge a new course free from colonialism's legacy and alleged foreign exploitation. Following the coup, political analysts and local media conjectured that Russia would become more involved in Burkina Faso's military policy. Some even suggested that Russian mercenaries might be hired to aid in the fight with jihadist groups.

Also, the burgeoning Pan-African sentiments that had spread across the continent were a manifestation of the rejection of neocolonialism. In an effort to oppose Western hegemony and advance an idea of African unity and independence, Traoré's military leadership of Burkina Faso joined a larger wave of Pan-African organizations. Burkina Faso was not alone in the frustrations that had resulted in Traoré's coup; they were a reflection of a broader desire among African countries to seek alternatives to Western-led interventions and to have greater control over their own destiny. As a result, many saw Traoré's activities as a component of a broader continental and regional movement for autonomy and opposition to neocolonial rule.

There were dangers associated with this departure from neocolonial influence, however. Burkinabé's economic and military requirements were still considerably dependent on outside partners, despite the fact that the majority of the population favored the notion of an independent foreign policy. Burkina Faso had to deal with severe security issues, and its military was not prepared to deal with the escalating insurgency on its own. Traoré would have to manage these difficulties, striking a balance between his aspirations for sovereignty and the realities of maintaining the nation's security and progress in a world still ruled by superpowers.

Traoré's Bold Stance Against French Military Presence

Captain Ibrahim Traoré made it plain that Burkina Faso would no longer tolerate French military involvement in its internal affairs as soon as he came to power. His choice to stand firm against French soldiers was motivated by more than simply security; it was also a desire to restore national sovereignty and put an end to a protracted period of outside meddling. As the Burkina Faso people got more and more irate about what they saw to be an antiquated and ineffectual system, Traoré emerged as the leader who was prepared to take immediate action in response to their demands.

Under the guise of supporting the battle against Islamist insurgencies, France has maintained a military presence in Burkina Faso for many years. Nevertheless, terrorist assaults have only become worse in spite of these initiatives, and large swaths of the nation were still ungoverned. Many Burkinabé thought that the French soldiers were solely there to further France's geopolitical objectives rather than to ensure Burkina Faso's security, and that they were either reluctant or incapable of defeating the militants. Having been on the front lines, Traoré was familiar with this dissatisfaction. He saw how troops relied on an outside force that did not put their fight first and were rushed into war with little supplies.

Traoré acted decisively shortly after taking over. His administration made a formal request for French soldiers to leave the country in January 2023. The request made it clear that Burkina Faso would no longer put up with an army from beyond its boundaries. Traoré moved quickly and refused to be constrained by prior accords that had left the nation reliant on outside powers, in contrast to previous presidents who were hesitant to publicly face France. The Burkinabé people overwhelmingly approved of the declaration, seeing it as a long-overdue step toward full independence.

The French army' departure was more than a token gesture. It signaled a change in Burkina Faso's foreign policy and security stance. Traoré said unequivocally that the nation will look for new allies that really cared about assisting it in the fight against terrorism and supported its sovereignty. Many conjectured that this action was a component of a larger plan to align with countries such as Russia, which had been increasing its influence in Africa. Through formal military pacts or unofficial collaboration, Traoré made it clear that Burkina Faso was amenable to new partnerships that put its interests ahead of those of other forces.

The administration took action to fortify the national army as French soldiers were about to depart. In order to encourage young men and women to enlist in the military and protect their nation, Traoré started recruiting efforts. Additionally, he stressed independence, calling on people to take charge of their own safety instead than relying on outside assistance. His statements demonstrated a strong sense of patriotism and served as a reminder to the populace that Burkina Faso's existence hinged on its own fortitude and solidarity.

More than just a political choice, Traoré's opposition to the French military presence represented a turning point in Burkina Faso's history. He gave his people their dignity back and put the country on the road to full sovereignty by opposing a former colonial power. It was unclear whether his plan would ultimately be successful, but one thing was for sure: Burkina Faso would no longer be a pawn in the hands of international forces under his leadership.

Realigning Burkina Faso's International Partnerships

Following the withdrawal of French troops from Burkina Faso, Ibrahim Traoré focused on restructuring the nation's international ties. Establishing alliances that put Burkina Faso's security and progress first, free from the meddling of former colonial countries, was his unambiguous objective. His search for new partners who respected the nation's sovereignty and were prepared to provide concrete assistance in the war on terrorism signaled a sea change in the nation's foreign policy.

A major change in Traoré's foreign policy was the improvement of relations with Russia. Burkina Faso started looking into more extensive military cooperation with Moscow, following the lead from neighbor Mali. This choice was not unexpected considering Russia's growing sway in West Africa, where nations fed up with Western meddling were looking for new allies. The open dialogue between Traoré's administration and Russian authorities demonstrated their willingness to provide military support, including training, equipment, and strategic collaboration. Despite the lack of official evidence, foreign observers continued to speculate about the potential of Russian mercenaries, like the Wagner Group, working in Burkina Faso.

In addition to military alliances, Traoré pursued political and commercial ties with other African countries. Although both Mali and Niger were ruled by military juntas that had turned away from Western influence, his administration promoted closer relations with both countries.

The rejection of foreign domination and the three countries' dedication to regional cooperation allowed them to find common ground while confronting comparable security concerns. This agreement sparked conversations about information sharing, cooperative military operations, and a counterterrorism strategy independent of Western powers.

Concurrently, Traoré increased diplomatic contacts with non-Western nations like China and Turkey. Burkina Faso saw a chance to capitalize on the infrastructure developments and trade agreements that had already allowed both countries to expand their influence in Africa. With its substantial investments in African economies, China offered a substitute for dependence on help from the West. Turkey has surfaced as a possible partner for military and economic cooperation, having been heavily engaged in defense and building projects around the continent.

Meanwhile, there was still tension in ties with Western countries, especially France and the

European Union. Under his leadership, Traoré blatantly broke earlier accords that had maintained Burkina Faso's reliance on French financial and military support. Even while diplomatic lines were still open, the nation was clearly heading in a new way. The increasing distance between Burkina Faso and its longstanding Western friends was highlighted by the French soldiers' departure and the halt of several European development initiatives.

Despite these adjustments, Traoré said that he wanted to redefine Burkina Faso's place in the world, not isolate the country. His strategy was practical; he looked for alliances that benefited his people rather than those that were imposed by outside forces. His goal in broadening Burkina Faso's coalitions was to make the country more autonomous and self-sufficient, free from the shackles of neocolonialism. His reorientation of diplomatic alliances was more than simply a change in approach; it was a daring proclamation that Burkina Faso will forge its own path in the world.

CHAPTER 5: THE SECURITY DILEMMA – FIGHTING FOR STABILITY

Strategies To Combat Terrorism And Insurgency

Ibrahim Traoré recognized that the continuous terrorist insurgency that had caused years of instability in Burkina Faso was one of the biggest obstacles the nation was facing. Extremist organizations had taken over large swaths of the country, causing thousands of people to leave their homes. Prior administrations had had difficulty controlling the violence and had mostly relied on foreign military support, with limited success. Determined to turn things around, Traoré unveiled a number of audacious plans to bolster national security, retake lost land, and bring stability back without relying on outside assistance.

His vigorous military recruiting push was one of his first significant actions. His administration urged the Burkinabé people to actively participate in the defense of their country on the grounds that the current army was overworked and ill-prepared. The appeal was answered by thousands of young men and women who were ready to enlist in the military and defend their nation. Alongside this massive hiring, the military leadership was reorganized to guarantee that the commanders were skilled, driven, and in line with Traoré's goal of a more robust national defense.

Traoré increased the role of citizen defense troops called the Volunteers for the Defense of the Homeland (VDP) in order to better empower local communities. Weapons, training, and logistical assistance were provided to these locally trained combatants, who were selected from towns and villages that had been directly impacted by terrorist assaults. The VDP personnel were able to carry out targeted operations more effectively than standard armed forces because they had a thorough understanding of the terrain and adversary movements. By bridging the divide between the rural populace and the central authority, this grassroots strategy promoted a united front against rebels.

The decentralization of military operations was another essential element of Traoré's plan. He made sure that regional commanders had more autonomy in making decisions rather than depending only on a single command organization headquartered in the capital. This adaptability made it possible to react to new threats more quickly and cut down on bureaucratic red tape that had previously impeded efficient action. Military troops were able to retake strategic regions that had been occupied by terrorists for a long time and conduct surprise offensives with a more flexible approach.

Traoré underlined the need of addressing the underlying roots of extremism in addition to military actions. Because of their restricted options, lack of education, and poverty, many young men have been lured into terrorist organizations. His administration launched social initiatives centered on education, vocational training, and job development in order to combat this. The goal was to lessen the attractiveness of joining armed organizations and the impact of extremist recruiters by giving young people other options.

Better intelligence cooperation and collection were also top priorities for Traoré's government. In order to follow terrorist movements, new surveillance equipment was developed, and attempts were made to improve regional collaboration with other nations who faced comparable concerns. By prohibiting rebels from exploiting national borders as safe havens, intelligence-sharing agreements with Mali and Niger made cross-border operations more effective.

Additionally, Traoré aimed to increase civilian-military confidence. Security force abuses in the past have stoked animosity and, in some situations, encouraged people to back extremist organizations. He put in place stringent accountability procedures to restore trust, making sure that troops and VDP combatants conducted their actions in an ethical manner. In order to promote collaboration rather than fear, his administration promoted communication between military authorities and local leaders.

Through these concerted measures, Traoré's approach aimed to secure Burkina Faso's citizens, restore its sovereignty, and reconstruct a country that could exist alone all in addition to combating terrorists. Although the fight against insurgency was far from done, the nation made great strides toward recovering authority and establishing a new course for peace and stability under his direction.

Strengthening The military And local defense initiatives

Ibrahim Traoré realized as soon as he took office that Burkina Faso's military was ill-prepared to deal with the magnitude of the terrorist insurgency engulfing the country. The military forces were overburdened and unable to retake significant areas of the nation from extremist organizations due to years of underfunding, dependence on foreign aid, and poor leadership. In order to create a self-sufficient national security framework that could protect Burkina Faso without relying on previous colonial powers, Traoré was determined to reverse this and gave top priority to bolstering the military and local defense forces.

Increasing military recruiting was one of his first significant actions. Thousands of young men and women who were ready to defend their nation responded to Traoré's government's statewide appeal for volunteers to join the armed services. The goal of this mass enrollment was to build a disciplined and driven army that was prepared to defend national sovereignty, not only to increase the number of soldiers. Training programs were stepped up to guarantee effectiveness, emphasizing counterinsurgency techniques, guerrilla warfare tactics, and rapid-response skills. Soldiers were ready to fight extremely mobile terrorist organizations in both asymmetrical and traditional combat.

Another goal was to provide the military with cutting-edge equipment and weaponry. Under Traoré's direction, Burkina Faso pursued new defense alliances with nations such as China, Russia, and Turkey in order to negotiate weapons agreements and get military assistance. Traoré sought for alternative suppliers who were prepared to provide weaponry, drones, and surveillance technology without political restrictions, in contrast to earlier governments that relied on France for military supplies. With the advent of these new tools, the military was better equipped to monitor and neutralize terrorist threats.

Traoré was aware, therefore, that the nation could not be secured by armed might alone. He increased the role of the Volunteers for the Defense of the Homeland (VDP), a local militia made up of people who had received training to defend their towns and villages against terrorist attacks, after realizing the strategic value of community-driven defense initiatives. The VDP, which had previously been condemned for having insufficient support and weapons, was reorganized under Traoré's presidency. To make sure they could maintain their own against militants, members received more training, stronger weaponry, and more logistical assistance.

Traoré's administration established a decentralized command structure in order to better incorporate local defense projects. In order to make sure that local defense units got the assistance they needed, military personnel were sent to collaborate closely with community leaders. Better coordination between the national army and citizen fighters as well as speedier reactions to terrorist threats were made possible by this partnership. Improved information exchange between local populations and military forces also made it easier to follow rebel movements and launch preemptive attacks against their hiding places.

The attention shifted to military morale as well. Traoré implemented policies to enhance troops' well-being, such as increased pay, access to healthcare, and awards for valiant combat. He made sure that troops stayed dedicated to the goal and did not feel abandoned by the state by resolving long-standing concerns among the military ranks.

There were still difficulties in spite of their attempts. The security forces of Burkina Faso continued to engage in cross-border operations against highly organized and well-armed terrorist organizations. A new age, however, was heralded by Traoré's focus on bolstering the military and enabling local defense projects, one in which Burkina Faso would take charge of its own security, depend on its own people, and struggle to recapture its territory free from outside intervention.

Regional Security Alliances With Mali And Niger

Ibrahim Traoré placed a high priority on regional collaboration after realizing that Burkina Faso's security situation could not be resolved in isolation. He established solid military ties with neighboring Mali and Niger. Terrorist organizations that operated across porous borders and took advantage of the lack of official presence in isolated regions posed a threat to all three of these Sahelian countries. Instead of depending on Western assistance, which had not succeeded, Traoré collaborated with Assimi Goïta of Mali and Abdourahamane Tchiani of Niger to create a cohesive plan for combating insurgency, safeguarding borders, and claiming sovereignty over their own regions.

An important turning point in this new regional security cooperation was the creation of the Alliance of Sahel States (AES). This coalition was formed by Traoré and the governments of Mali and Niger as a substitute for military coalitions supported by the West, including the G5 Sahel, that had not been able to stop terrorism. By emphasizing coordinated military operations, information sharing, and mutual defense, the AES made sure that terrorist organizations could no longer utilize national borders as a means of eluding security authorities. Because these countries were refusing to follow orders from other sources and instead deciding to manage their security on their own terms, the alliance also made a political statement.

The unified military plan for carrying out cross-border operations was a crucial feature of this collaboration. Because national militaries had little authority outside of their boundaries, rebels used to strike in one nation and then flee into another. Security forces in Burkina Faso,

Mali, and Niger were given more latitude under the AES framework to carry out coordinated operations, track terrorists into nearby areas, and provide reinforcements as necessary. This degree of military collaboration improved the battle against Islamist organizations and led to a more coordinated reaction to security risks.

The alliance placed a strong emphasis on information sharing in addition to military cooperation. The three countries set up safe lines of communication between their military ministries because they understood that fighting militants required quick and reliable intelligence. This made it possible to get up-to-date information on enemy movements, possible terrorist hiding places, and weapons trafficking routes. Instead than just responding to events after they happened, any nation's military might foresee assaults and carry out preemptive strikes with this improved cooperation.

Traoré and his colleagues saw foreign economic influence as another kind of control, so in addition to their immediate security concerns, they also aimed to lessen their reliance on France and the West. The alliance looked for methods to improve infrastructure, commerce, and resource sharing between the three countries, going beyond military cooperation to include economic cooperation. Building resilience against international economic pressures and sanctions imposed after military takeovers in the area was the aim of strengthening commercial links.

The AES had difficulties even though it put up a brave front. These countries had to create new regional economic policies to maintain stability after leaving the Economic Community of West African States (ECOWAS) due to political unrest. Furthermore, Western governments were skeptical of the alliance, particularly as these nations strengthened their ties with Russia and other non-Western allies. Traoré was steadfast in his resolve to make sure Burkina Faso had trustworthy partners that put regional security and sovereignty ahead of outside interests.

Traoré reduced Burkina Faso's dependency on foreign military troops while solidifying Burkina Faso's role in the war against terrorism by fortifying relations with Mali and Niger. The AES was more than simply a military agreement; it was a proclamation of regional self-determination and independence from neocolonial domination. Under his leadership, Burkina Faso was fighting as a unified front, determined to regain control of its future and territory, rather than as an isolated nation.

CHAPTER 6: THE PAN-AFRICAN DREAM – A UNITED AFRICA

Traoré's Vision For African Economic And Political Independence

Ibrahim Traoré has been a vocal supporter of African countries' independence from foreign political and economic domination. He feels that if African nations continue to rely on former colonial powers for economic guidance, military protection, and financial assistance, they would never be able to attain full sovereignty. Self-reliance, regional collaboration, and the rejection of the structures that have kept Africa under foreign domination for many years are at the heart of his worldview.

Breaking away from Western financial frameworks that have traditionally constrained Africa's progress is at the core of Traoré's economic philosophy. He has publicly attacked the CFA franc, which is still under French authority and is utilized by a number of West African nations. According to Traoré, this monetary system prevents countries from having control over their own financial policies and is an instrument of economic exploitation. He has backed talks to create alternative currency systems that would let West African nations run their economy without interference from the European Union.

Traoré sees a Burkina Faso that uses its natural resources for national development, regardless of currency issues. Burkina Faso, like many other African nations, has abundant gold and other resources, but because of foreign mining contracts that benefit multinational businesses, it does not gain much from these riches. Under his direction, attempts have been made to renegotiate these agreements so that a larger portion of the revenues remain domestically and are used to fund healthcare, education, and infrastructure. In an effort to increase employment and national output, he has also pushed domestic businesses to process raw resources rather than exporting them at a discount.

Traoré has advocated for greater political union among African countries. He contends that by keeping African nations apart, Western powers have been able to retain control over each one more easily. He has opposed this by advocating for more regional cooperation in commerce, governance, and security issues. This approach is shown in his relationship with Mali and Niger, two nations working to establish institutions free from Western influence.

Furthermore, Traoré sees Africa free from military reliance on other countries. He feels that Africans should be in charge of their own security, free from the meddling of former colonial rulers who often use military assistance as a tool of control. His decision to remove French soldiers from Burkina Faso made it very evident that his nation would no longer be protected by foreign powers. In order to combat threats together, he has instead focused on bolstering internal security forces and establishing military partnerships with regional allies.

His long-term goals include youth empowerment and education. Traoré is aware that a people with knowledge and skills is necessary for real freedom. He has discussed changing educational institutions to emphasize information that directly advances African development rather than following European models. He intends to provide the next generation the resources they need to advance the continent by making investments in agricultural production, vocational training, and technological innovation.

Traoré's leadership marks a daring departure from previous strategies that bound African countries to Western interests. His dedication to military independence, regional unity, and economic self-sufficiency represents a shift in course for Burkina Faso and maybe the continent. He is one of several African leaders who are committed to redefining Africa's role in the world using principles of self-determination, dignity, and real sovereignty.

Strengthening Ties With Revolutionary Leaders Across The Continent

Ibrahim Traoré is aware that Burkina Faso's battle for independence and self-determination is not unique. In an effort to achieve full political and economic independence, leaders and groups across Africa are resisting neocolonial influence. Understanding the strength of unity, Traoré has made a concerted effort to form partnerships with leaders who share his vision of an Africa free and independent. His objective is to establish a continental network of revolutionary leaders who put African interests ahead of imperialist dominance.

Assimi Goïta of Mali is one of Traoré's most ardent supporters in this endeavor; he has likewise resisted Western meddling and strived for independence. Terrorism, economic exploitation, and pressure from Western-backed organizations that try to control their policies are issues that both presidents have had to deal with. Traoré and Goïta have shown their commitment to economic cooperation, mutual defense, and opposing foreign military involvement via their alliance in the Alliance of Sahel States (AES). Their cooperation makes it quite evident that Africans, not outside forces, will determine the continent's destiny.

Mamady Doumbouya of Guinea is another important member of Traoré's revolutionary network. Similar to Traoré, Doumbouya has advocated for African nations to manage their own resources and choose their own political course. The two presidents have discussed economic changes that encourage commerce between African countries and lessen reliance on Western financial institutions. They want to separate from economic structures that maintain Africa's reliance by fortifying these connections.

Traoré has turned to leaders in Southern and Eastern Africa who support Pan-African unity and opposition to foreign dominance in addition to those in West Africa. He has been influenced by the policies of Thomas Sankara, the famous revolutionary leader of Burkina Faso, and he sees remnants of that legacy in modern leaders like Julius Malema of South Africa, who advocates for radical economic change in favor of African ownership, and Abiy Ahmed of Ethiopia, who has pushed for African-led conflict resolution.

State leaders are not the only people Traoré is reaching out to. Additionally, he has established connections with intellectuals, youth activists, and grassroots groups around the continent who share his vision for African independence. He has backed programs that promote African heritage, independence, and resistance to outside exploitation because he understands the need for ideological unity. He is aware that cultural changes that give Africans the confidence to take charge of their own affairs are also necessary for political revolutions.

Global powers have taken note of his attempts to bring revolutionary leaders together, however. These partnerships have been seen by Western countries, especially France, as a direct threat to their historical hegemony over Africa. The new generation of African presidents has been criticized via media narratives, diplomatic pressure, and sanctions. Knowing that a divided Africa would still be ruled from the outside, Traoré is unwavering.

Traoré is promoting the notion that Africa's fight for independence must be a joint effort by forging close relationships with revolutionary leaders around the continent. Africa can only regain its riches, security, and political destiny by means of regional and continental cooperation; no one nation can attain real sovereignty on its own. His actions are a major step toward a new age when African countries stand together in their common struggle for independence and opposition to neocolonial rule.

Advocating For Self-Reliance And Intra-African Cooperation

According to Ibrahim Traoré, Africa's capacity to stand on its own two feet economically and politically is the key to its eventual full independence. African countries have depended on international organizations, Western financial institutions, and foreign assistance for decades. These organizations often impose rules that benefit outside interests rather than the African people. In order to create a bright future, African nations must fully manage their own resources, industries, and political structures, according to Traoré, who has become a vocal opponent of this reliance.

Economic self-reliance is central to his worldview. Traoré has advocated for a change from an export-based economy that enriches multinational firms while maintaining the poverty cycle in African countries. He supports value-added enterprises that process raw materials on the continent instead, giving locals employment and money. Rich in agricultural goods and gold, Burkina Faso has a history of exporting these resources without fully using their potential. Under Traoré's direction, attempts have been made to renegotiate mining contracts and support indigenous companies capable of producing and refining final items instead of sending cheap raw materials overseas.

Traoré emphasizes the value of regional and continental collaboration in addition to national self-sufficiency. He contends that commerce among African nations is more advantageous than depending only on markets in North America or Europe. His idea is in line with the African Continental Free commerce Area (AfCFTA), which seeks to increase intra-African commerce by lowering obstacles. With an emphasis on cooperative energy projects, local marketplaces that support African companies, and shared infrastructure projects, he has pushed for deeper economic linkages between Burkina

Faso and its neighbors, including Mali and Niger.

Traoré also advocates for independence in the agricultural sector. He has underlined the importance of food security and promoted measures to boost local production and lessen reliance on imports. Like many African countries, Burkina Faso possesses rich terrain that, with the right use, could support its people without the need for food imports. Traoré wants to make his country food secure by investing in irrigation systems, modern agricultural methods, and local supply chains. He also wants to encourage commerce with other African countries that have similar objectives.

Another key component of his vision is energy independence. French-controlled power networks are among the foreign energy sources that Burkina Faso and a large portion of West Africa have long relied on. Traoré has backed projects aimed at using Africa's enormous renewable energy potential by creating alternative energy sources including solar and hydroelectric electricity. He hopes to lessen dependency on outside vendors and increase the affordability and accessibility of power for Burkinabé residents by investing in domestic energy generation.

In terms of politics, Traoré supports closer regional ties in order to lessen Africa's need for institutions run by the West. He thinks that institutions like ECOWAS, which are sometimes swayed by outside interests, have not been able to meet the actual requirements of African countries. He is dedicated to African-led government institutions that put local interests ahead of foreign directives, as seen by his support for alternative regional alliances like the Alliance of Sahel States (AES).

Traoré's appeal for independence is about empowerment rather than loneliness. He is aware that Africa has the people, resources, and expertise necessary to prosper independently of outside intervention. His support for intra-African collaboration stems from his conviction that African countries must have faith in and assist one another in order to use their combined capabilities to create a future free from reliance on outside forces. He sees Africa regaining its proper position on the international scene and controlling its own destiny via economic, political, and strategic unification.

CHAPTER 7: CHALLENGES FROM WITHIN AND ABROAD

Opposition From Political Elites And Economic Struggles

Ibrahim Traoré's vision for Burkina Faso's sovereignty has been threatened by economic difficulties and strong resistance from long-standing political elites since he came to office in September 2022. Long-standing power systems that favored a privileged few have been upended by his swift drive for economic self-reliance, military reform, and independence from outside interference. Because they see his initiatives as a danger to their interests, former politicians, corporate leaders, and international organizations have begun to oppose him.

Members of the former administration and military officials who supported the overthrown leader, Paul-Henri Sandaogo Damiba, were among the first to express political opposition. Internal conflicts arose among the leading military groups after the September 2022 coup. Fearing that Traoré's swift changes might lead to diplomatic and economic isolation, several senior commanders questioned his leadership style. There were even countercoup rumors by early 2023, according to tales of discontent among military factions who were reluctant to cut all connections with Western nations.

The political elite of Burkina Faso, many of whom had strong ties to France and Western organizations, saw Traoré's anti-neocolonial initiatives as an outright assault on their financial interests. Deals with global firms have long benefitted these elites, some of whom held significant positions in areas including finance, telecommunications, and mining. Business tycoons who depended on foreign alliances for their earnings fiercely opposed Traoré's 2023 efforts to renegotiate mining contracts, insisting that more of Burkina Faso's gold riches belong to the domestic economy.

Traoré's leadership has also been put to the test by economic difficulties. France and the

European Union reacted economically to the 2023 decision to withdraw French forces and shift toward alliances with nations like Russia and Turkey. Western assistance, which had previously made up a significant amount of Burkina Faso's budget, was trimmed or decreased in 2023 and 2024 as a result of economic hardship. This led to acute financial hardship, making it difficult to finance infrastructure projects, military operations, and government programs.

Burkina Faso's economic circumstances were made even more difficult by sanctions imposed by the Economic Community of West African States (ECOWAS) in 2023 and 2024. Western-influenced ECOWAS placed economic and diplomatic constraints, claiming that the return to civilian governance was unclear. Ordinary residents' lives were made more difficult by these restrictions, which had an impact on commerce, raised prices, and caused gasoline shortages. Traoré persisted in his position in spite of this, opposing outside demands for governance and urging African countries to fend against economic extortion.

In 2024, the public's annoyance with economic woes increased as increasing food costs and inflation made everyday living more challenging. In Burkina Faso, some of Traoré's detractors blamed the country's economic downturn on his combative foreign policy. His supporters countered that in order to attain long-term independence and stability, the short-term hardships required sacrifices. Traoré started new industrial and agricultural projects with the goal of increasing domestic output and lowering reliance on imports in order to solve economic issues.

Notwithstanding these challenges, Traoré is steadfast in his resolve to transform Burkina Faso's economy and liberate it from foreign-run structures. Political elites who have lost their power continue to oppose him, but he is resilient enough to overcome these obstacles because of his tremendous grassroots support among Burkinabé citizens and his expanding coalitions with other African revolutionary leaders. Under his leadership, the fight is not just against rebels but also against those who want to keep Africa under the rule of outside powers.

Foreign Media Narratives, Diplomatic Difficulties, And Western sanctions

Ibrahim Traoré soon found himself at conflict with Western countries as he stepped up his demands for Burkina Faso's sovereignty. This resulted in a number of diplomatic issues, economic penalties, and unfavorable representations in the media. Former colonial countries and their allies reacted forcefully to his government's 2023 and 2024 decisions to cut military links with France, reject Western meddling, and strengthen partnerships with non-traditional partners.

The economic sanctions enforced by the European Union and several Western financial institutions in 2023 were among the first and most significant repercussions. The government money, security support, and development aid that had long been used as leverage to sway African regimes were the targets of these sanctions. Western nations wanted to put pressure on Traoré to change his mind and bring Burkina Faso back into line with their strategic objectives, so they stopped providing financial assistance. The nation could no longer accept help that came with political stipulations that threatened its independence, Traoré said.

Burkina Faso was subject to further diplomatic isolation in addition to economic penalties. France removed its ambassador from Ouagadougou in 2023 as tensions between the two countries increased. Similar diplomatic downgrades were subsequently made by other European nations that had previously maintained tight ties with the previous administrations of Burkina Faso. Travel advisories from Western embassies deterred foreign investment and made it more difficult for Burkina Faso to negotiate international trade agreements.

ECOWAS contributed to diplomatic conflicts as well, often under the sway of Western interests. Burkina Faso, Mali, and Niger were criticized by the regional group in 2023 and early 2024 for departing from their long-standing partnerships with Western countries. Traoré, Assimi Goïta of Mali, and the leadership of Niger originally resisted ECOWAS's attempts to persuade the three Sahel nations to maintain their connections with France and the West. Burkina Faso formally broke from ECOWAS in early 2024 to align more closely with other regional institutions like the Alliance of Sahel States (AES), which placed a higher priority on economic cooperation and security free from Western meddling.

The way the world saw Traoré and his administration was greatly influenced by foreign media. Western media sources often portrayed his rule as autocratic and characterized his actions as irresponsible and detrimental to the stability of Burkina Faso. Reports often overstated domestic problems, depicting the nation as in anarchy under his leadership while neglecting the past inadequacies of Western-backed governments that had failed to reduce terrorism or enhance the economy.

Major Western newspapers' headlines sometimes portrayed Traoré as an extreme or a Russian puppet, implying that his rejection of French influence was motivated by outside manipulation rather than by national interest. Western capitals were alarmed by his 2023 and 2024 intentions to deepen relations with Russia and Turkey, accusing Burkina Faso of siding with anti-Western forces. These stories attempted to undermine his administration and provide justification for any outside interference or ongoing financial pressure.

Traoré received a lot of support from intellectuals, young activists, and Pan-African organizations around the continent in spite of these representations. Many believed that the assaults by the Western media were a logical response to an African leader who defied the conventional wisdom of submission and dependence. Social media platforms turned into a battlefield where African voices contested popular narratives by drawing attention to the hypocrisy of Western countries that had long backed corrupt regimes and were now denouncing a leader that was attempting to become self-sufficient.

Instead of retreating, Traoré mobilized support for Burkina Faso's independence by using these diplomatic issues. He improved ties with other international allies, obtaining military and economic collaboration that lessened the nation's need for the West. In order to prevent sanctions and diplomatic isolation from crippling the country, Burkina Faso inked trade and security agreements with China, Russia, and Turkey by the middle of 2024.

Traoré has stuck to his idea in the face of fierce resistance from Western governments, international media, and business organizations. Although the fight for Burkina Faso's independence has not been simple, he is unfazed by outside forces and committed to demonstrating that Africa can function independently of outside authority.

Internal Resistance And Governance Obstacles

Ibrahim Traoré has continued to have widespread support from Burkinabé residents, but internal opposition and governance issues have plagued his administration. Opposition from within Burkina Faso has surfaced from a variety of groups as he continues to carry out his vision of political sovereignty, security, and self-reliance. These groups include members of the military, some civilian groups who are dubious of his strategy, and even some members of the former political elite. One of his biggest challenges has been handling these conflicts while leading a country beset by security concerns and economic hardships.

The political class that profited from earlier administrations is one of the main drivers of internal opposition. The government of Burkina Faso had close relations to France and Western organizations before Traoré's ascent to power, and many of its leaders had financial and personal interests connected to these alliances. His quest for nationalized businesses, renegotiation of mining contracts, and rejection of Western influence put these elites' economic advantages in jeopardy. In order to thwart reforms, finance opposition organizations, and sow discord among government institutions, a few former ministers, businesspeople, and bureaucrats have clandestinely worked against his administration.

There have also been pockets of opposition inside the military. Even though many subordinate officers backed Traoré's ascent, not every branch of the military shares his vision. Some commanders have been reluctant to accept the move away from foreign military alliances, especially those who received French training or had frequent contact with Western troops. Rumors of possible coup attempts surfaced in 2023 and 2024, and certain groups expressed discontent, believing that Burkina Faso's military's ability to operate may be weakened by its increasing isolation from Western allies. In order to combat this, Traoré has made it a top priority to bolster regional defense programs and eliminate security forces members who could endanger his authority.

Another difficulty has been civilian governance. Even though Traoré is well-liked by the public, especially young people, several groups have voiced worries about the persisting security situation and the sluggish rate of economic recovery. Significant financial pressure was caused by the 2023 and 2024 sanctions imposed by the EU, France, and ECOWAS, as well as the removal of Western funding. These measures made it more difficult for the government to invest in infrastructure, pay wages, and provide services. Teachers, healthcare professionals, and civil officials are among the public sector employees who have sometimes expressed their dissatisfaction with late payments and resource shortages, sparking demonstrations and strikes.

The ongoing danger of terrorism and insurgency is another major governance challenge. Extremist organizations continue to assault communities, security personnel, and vital infrastructure, making Burkina Faso one of the Sahel's most vulnerable nations. The war on terrorism is far from done, even if Traoré has stepped up military operations and strengthened ties with Mali and Niger via the Alliance of Sahel States (AES) in 2024. His government has been under a great deal of strain to manage internal security while juggling political and economic issues.

Traoré also has trouble striking a balance between the reality of a military-led transition and calls for democratic rule. There are demands for a clear path to civilian control, even if many residents accept his leadership. His detractors contend that Burkina Faso runs the danger of slipping into protracted military rule in the absence of a clear election schedule. However, Traoré has maintained that any meaningful return to civilian control cannot be carried out until peace and security are established.

Traoré keeps moving ahead in spite of these internal challenges by depending on the support of pro-sovereignty movements across Africa as well as his grassroots supporters. Fighting insurgencies, stopping political sabotage, handling economic hardship, and maintaining public confidence all need careful balance under his leadership. How well he handles the internal opposition and guides Burkina Faso toward long-term stability and independence will determine if he can overcome these governance obstacles and cement his reputation as a transformative leader.

CHAPTER 8: MOBILIZING THE YOUTH AND GRASSROOTS MOVEMENTS

The Role Of Young People In Burkina Faso's Revolution

Young people were in the front of the revolution that brought Ibrahim Traoré to power, and they have been essential in Burkina Faso's political transition. Burkina Faso's youth have been essential in forming the nation's new period, from large-scale demonstrations against ineffective leadership to their active involvement in security, governance, and economic transformation. They have been vital partners in Traoré's fight for national sovereignty because of their vigor, dissatisfaction with previous administrations, and longing for ultimate independence.

The inability of earlier administrations to meet their demands was a major factor in the youth's support for Traoré. Many young Burkinabés believed the government had abandoned them prior to his ascent to power in September 2022. They had few alternatives for a brighter future because of high unemployment, inadequate educational possibilities, and deteriorating security circumstances. Many young people have been further uprooted by the rise in terrorist-related violence since 2015, which has kept them in poverty and limited their opportunities for economic progress. They immediately trusted Traoré when he showed up as a leader who tackled these issues head-on.

Social media developed as an effective mobilizing tool. Young activists mobilized support for Burkina Faso's independence from foreign rule and disseminated messages of resistance against neocolonial influence during 2022 and 2023 using social media sites like Facebook, Twitter, and WhatsApp. Youth-led protests demanding an end to Western exploitation gained popularity as online campaigns denounced France's economic dominance and military presence. Hashtags such as #TraoreGeneration and #FreeBurkina emerged to represent a new spirit of revolt. In addition to influencing public opinion, this internet activism assisted in refuting unfavorable international media representations of Traoré's leadership.

Young people went to the streets in addition to engaging in online activism. Following Traoré's ascent to power, hundreds of young Burkinabés took part in anti-French demonstrations, calling for the evacuation of French soldiers and foreign-owned companies that were depleting the nation's resources. Many saw Traoré's historic move to evacuate French military soldiers in early 2023 as a clear win for agitation driven by young people.

Young people have played a significant role in Burkina Faso's security initiatives in addition to their political involvement. Traoré started volunteer defense projects (VDPs) in 2023 and 2024 to encourage young men and women to join local defense forces in response to the nation's ongoing threats by extremist organizations. Thousands participated in these programs and were equipped with weapons and training to defend their villages. Their participation has improved national security and shown the younger generation a newfound sense of patriotism.

Youth engagement has been equally important in terms of the economy. Traoré's philosophy of economic freedom has been adopted by local innovators and young entrepreneurs who understand the value of independence. The government implemented laws in 2024 that gave youth-led businesses priority, especially in the fields of technology, renewable energy, and agriculture. Young people are demonstrating that Burkina Faso can prosper without heavily depending on foreign help by investing in local enterprises.

The goals of the younger generation are embodied by Traoré himself. He broke the long-standing pattern of older, Western-aligned politicians ruling African governments by becoming the youngest leader in history at the age of 34. Millions of young Burkinabés now see politics as a means of bringing about significant change, and his youthfulness, enthusiasm, and direct interaction with the populace have made him approachable.

Young people continue to confront several obstacles despite their critical role, such as financial hardships, limited educational opportunities, and the dangers of violence. Nonetheless, they are more politically active than ever under Traoré's direction. Their ongoing action, tenacity, and will to create an independent Burkina Faso will shape the nation's destiny, even if the revolution they helped spark is far from done.

Economic And Educational Measures To Empower The Next Generation

Understanding that Burkina Faso's youth hold the key to its future, Ibrahim Traoré has made economic empowerment and education a top priority. In order to enable young people to contribute to the growth of the country independently of outside assistance or intervention, his administration has started projects to improve the educational system, provide access to vocational training, and establish economic possibilities. These policies stem from the conviction that Burkina Faso's youth must be given the tools and resources to propel the nation forward in order for it to attain real sovereignty.

Addressing the serious flaws in the school system was one of Traoré's first actions after taking office in 2022. Underfunding, inadequate facilities, and restricted access to high-quality educational resources have plagued Burkina

Faso's educational system for many years. Furthermore, hundreds of schools had to close due to terrorist assaults in rural regions, depriving many young people of an education. The National Education Recovery Plan, which Traoré's administration introduced in 2023 and 2024, aimed to increase public education financing, reopen schools in areas damaged by violence, and lessen reliance on foreign-controlled curriculum that propagated neocolonial ideals.

The advancement of African-centered education was a key component of this educational revolution. Policies to integrate Burkina Faso's history, culture, and revolutionary leaders particularly Thomas Sankarainto school curricula were instituted under Traoré's government. This action was intended to foster a sense of patriotism and guarantee that future generations recognized the value of independence and Pan-African solidarity. In order to provide students the practical skills they need to build local industries, there was also a drive to improve the teaching of science, technology, engineering, and mathematics (STEM), as well as agriculture and entrepreneurship.

In 2023 and 2024, Traoré started a number of business and vocational training initiatives to address young unemployment. In order to provide young people practical training in industries including mechanics, construction, agriculture, and renewable energy, the government made investments in technical and vocational education institutions (TVETs) all around the nation. By encouraging talents that may directly contribute to the nation's economic independence, these programs aimed to lessen reliance on white-collar occupations. In order to ensure that Burkina Faso could depend on its own workforce, Traoré sought to decrease the demand for imported labor and goods by emphasizing trade skills and industrial growth.

In terms of the economy, the Traoré government established youth empowerment funds in 2023, offering grants and low-interest loans to young business people wishing to launch ventures in important industries including manufacturing, technology, and agriculture. In order to promote youth involvement in agriculture, a field that had long been neglected by younger generations, the government also gave land grants and agricultural supplies. By 2024, more youth-led agribusinesses had been established as a result of these initiatives, increasing food security and decreasing dependency on imports.

The reorganization of Burkina Faso's mining sector was another significant economic change. In order to guarantee that local communities, not multinational firms, would profit from the nation's abundant natural resources, Traoré's government took the step to nationalize a section of the gold mining industry. Through government-sponsored cooperative mining initiatives, where earnings were put back into infrastructure and education, young people were encouraged to work in this industry.

Traoré's economic policy placed a strong emphasis on regional commercial integration. In

2024, Burkina Faso joined the Alliance of Sahel States (AES) alongside Mali and Niger in an effort to establish a cooperative economic framework that gave intra-African trade and industrial growth first priority. By supporting exports and regional alliances, Traoré's administration urged young entrepreneurs to access markets outside of Burkina Faso.

Despite advancements, difficulties still exist. Obstacles still exist because of the political opposition from established elites and the aftereffects of Western economic sanctions. However, as more young people actively participate in rebuilding their nation, the youth-led movement for economic self-reliance is gaining traction. Traoré's policies represent a dramatic shift from the past by providing Burkina Faso's young with the knowledge, abilities, and resources necessary to take charge of their own destiny, one that is independent of other influences and consistent with the ideals of real sovereignty..

Building A Sustainable Model Of Leadership For The Future

Ibrahim Traoré is aware that his leadership alone cannot bring about significant change in Burkina Faso. He has aggressively sought methods to create a sustainable style of government that places a premium on accountability, self-reliance, and young involvement in decision-making in order to ensure long-term stability and independence. Creating institutions and mechanisms that can preserve Burkina Faso's sovereignty and guarantee a new generation of capable, patriotic leaders is the main goal of his vision, which goes beyond his term in office.

Breaking the cycle of erratic leadership and military takeovers that have defined Burkina Faso's history has been one of Traoré's biggest problems. He has made it clear time and time again that his administration is a transitional leadership that aims to establish long-term political stability rather than just military rule.

Traoré has maintained that the goal is to restore security, carry out important reforms, and then switch to a leadership structure that really serves the people, in contrast to past presidents who held onto power permanently. This strategy has necessitated depoliticizing the military, restructuring government institutions, and developing a governance framework that guards against outside influence.

Promoting grassroots democracy has been a fundamental component of his approach. His government implemented community governance programs in 2023 and 2024, enabling local residents to actively participate in running their own affairs. Traoré seeks to guarantee that political power is shared among the populace rather than centralized in a single leader by strengthening traditional leaders, youth organizations, and civil society groups. Thomas Sankara's concept of participatory democracy, in which people actively participate in national affairs rather than acting as passive onlookers, serves as the model's inspiration.

Traoré has also placed a strong emphasis on leadership development programs for aspiring politicians, activists, and military commanders in an effort to fortify the political system even further. His administration has established patriotic leadership schools that emphasize Pan-Africanist philosophy, anti-corruption training, and economic self-sufficiency in recognition of the fact that past regimes often lacked capable, independent-minded officials. Instead of pursuing personal gain or foreign interests, these initiatives aim to create a new generation of leaders dedicated to national sovereignty and progress.

Economic self-sufficiency is another essential component in creating a sustainable leadership style. Burkina Faso cannot achieve full political independence without economic independence, as Traoré has said. In order to guarantee that future presidents would inherit a country that is in control of its own resources, his administration has moved to safeguard important sectors like mining, agriculture, and energy. He hopes to minimize the capacity of outside forces to affect or undermine Burkina Faso's leadership in the future by lowering reliance on outside assistance.

Restructuring the military's involvement in politics has been one of Traoré's most contentious but essential changes. He has advocated for a permanent division between military and civilian rule, even if his leadership started as a military incursion. His objective is to establish a professional, nationalist military that serves the people rather than meddling in politics, in contrast to previous juntas that just swapped over one dictatorship for another. In order to do this, he has put in place stringent codes of conduct, loyalty assessments, and leadership development for officers, guaranteeing that future military commanders support national sovereignty objectives rather than those of foreign powers.

Traoré is also aware of how crucial regional partnerships are to maintaining stable leadership over the long run. Burkina Faso is assisting in the formation of a unified front against neo colonial influence and regime transitions supported by the West via the Alliance of Sahel States (AES) alongside Mali and Niger. He intends to stop foreign powers from using economic or military pressure to topple succeeding regimes by strengthening relations with other like-minded countries.

There are still difficulties in spite of his efforts. The political climate in Burkina Faso is still precarious, and resistance from both domestic and foreign elites poses a danger to advancement. But compared to previous leaders, Traoré's strategy is essentially different. His priorities include establishing institutions, preparing the next generation of leaders, and making sure Burkina Faso's government system is impervious to corruption and outside influence rather than pursuing personal power.

In the end, Traoré's legacy will be assessed not just on his leadership but also on his ability to provide the framework for a Burkina Faso that is really autonomous and self-sufficient. Future generations will inherit a country free from outside influence, a government answerable to the people, and a leadership style that guarantees political stability and economic growth for years to come if his vision is carried out.

CHAPTER 9: THE LEGACY OF A REVOLUTIONARY LEADER

Ibrahim Traoré's Impact On Burkina Faso And Africa's Future

Under Ibrahim Traoré's leadership, Burkina Faso has seen substantial transformation, and his leadership has had a profound impact on Africa's future. His policies on economic independence, security, and governance have changed the political climate of his nation and served as an example for other African countries. His fearless opposition to outside interference, emphasis on regional collaboration, and dedication to national independence have made Burkina Faso a symbol of African resistance and advancement.

Restoring Burkina Faso's sovereignty has been one of his greatest achievements. Prior to his tenure, the nation was largely dependent on outside forces for both economic and security assistance. By driving out French troops and looking for new alliances, Traoré altered this.

His resolve to establish a self-sufficient defense system was shown by his decision to withdraw foreign forces. In addition to boosting national pride, this action prompted other African countries to reevaluate their dependence on former colonial powers.

Traoré has made economic independence a top priority in addition to security changes. In particular, he has pushed for Burkina Faso to profit from its own resources, especially in the mining industry. In an effort to retain more money domestically, the government has renegotiated agreements with international businesses under his direction. By supporting regional industry, his programs increase the growth prospects of Burkinabé companies. He has established a model for economic self-sufficiency that other African countries might emulate by decreasing reliance on outside assistance.

Regional relations have also changed as a result of his leadership. Traoré has been essential in fortifying relations with other nations dealing with comparable issues. He has contributed to the development of a unified front against terrorism and foreign meddling by establishing the Alliance of Sahel States (AES) with Mali and Niger. By encouraging collaboration in commerce, security, and governance, this alliance demonstrates that African countries are capable of resolving their own issues independently of outside assistance. Stronger African-led solutions to regional instability have been bolstered by his influence.

Beyond economy and security, Traoré's leadership has motivated youth across Africa. Being among the youngest presidents of state on the continent, he exemplifies a new leadership style that puts the interests of the country ahead of outside pressure. His ascent to power has inspired a lot of young Africans to become involved in politics and strive for independent government. His approach to leadership, which involves open communication with the public and open decision-making, has raised the bar for political responsibility.

In order to provide a solid basis for Burkina Faso's future, Traoré's policies likewise place a major emphasis on education and skill development. He is setting up the nation for long-term stability by encouraging industrial development, agricultural innovation, and technical training. His goal is to create a system that will allow future generations to prosper without outside interference, not only bring about change right now.

His influence on Africa's political trajectory goes beyond Burkina Faso. His administration is seen by several politicians and activists around the continent as an example of how to prioritize local development and lessen reliance on outside assistance. His acts have upended established power structures and shown that African nations are capable of claiming their independence and determining their own future.

Under Ibrahim Traoré's direction, Burkina Faso has changed and a new vision for Africa's future has been established. His governance, economic, and security measures have fortified his nation and paved the way for independence. His strategy may usher in a new age of African freedom and unification if it continues to garner support.

Lessons From His Leadership And The Resurgence Of Pan-Africanism

Burkina Faso and the larger African continent have learned a lot from Ibrahim Traoré's leadership. His audacious stance on regional cooperation, economic independence, and governance has sparked a fresh wave of nationalist groups and rekindled debates about Pan-Africanism. His leadership is evidence that African countries can take charge of their own fate, rejecting outside influence and promoting solidarity among themselves.

The value of independence in security and governance is among the most important lessons to be learned from Traoré's leadership. He has shown that African countries can protect themselves if they invest in their own military infrastructure by driving out foreign military troops and lowering reliance on Western intervention. His security strategy, which emphasizes regional partnerships, national military bolstering, and local defense projects, has become a template for other African nations facing comparable turmoil. Following his lead, nations like Mali and Niger have prioritized domestic security options over international military intervention.

The need for economic sovereignty is yet another important lesson. To regain control of Burkina Faso's natural resources, especially in the mining industry, Traoré has taken decisive action. He has opposed the exploitative economic models pushed by foreign powers by making sure that the wealth created from the nation's resources serves its citizens. His programs emphasize how crucial it is for African countries to bargain fairly for their resources rather than letting multinational firms embezzle their riches. This strategy has spurred debates about how African countries may develop economies that benefit their own people rather than advancing the interests of foreign powers.

Additionally, Traoré's leadership strengthens the influence of young people in politics. He defied the convention of older, more established politicians ruling African countries by taking government at the age of only 34. His ascent to power has shown that the younger generation is capable of enacting significant change by motivating young people to take on leadership roles and participate in political engagement. He is seen as a role model by many African youths, who are inspired to take charge of their nations' destiny instead of waiting for the established political elite to reform.

Additionally, his administration has highlighted regional collaboration as essential to Africa's development. Traoré has forged closer relationships with other nations dealing with comparable issues rather than turning to previous colonial overlords for assistance and support. A new kind of Pan-African solidarity based on common development objectives and mutual protection is shown by the formation of the Alliance of Sahel States (AES) with Mali and Niger. His leadership serves as a reminder that African nations may resolve their differences by cooperating instead of depending on outside forces that often put their own interests first.

One of Traoré's most important accomplishments was the revival of Pan-Africanism under his direction. He has promoted a unified Africa free from neocolonialism, reviving the ideas of figures such as Kwame Nkrumah, Patrice Lumumba, and Thomas Sankara. His policies are in line with the fundamental tenets of Pan-Africanism, which include regional unification, military self-sufficiency, and economic independence. Calls for a new political and economic structure that puts African interests ahead of foreign agendas have gained momentum thanks to his influence.

His leadership demonstrates that strengthening internal institutions, encouraging self-sufficiency, and promoting international unity are key to Africa's future. A new age of real independence, where African riches benefit Africans and national interests, rather than foreign influence, drive government, may dawn on the continent if more politicians adopt his vision. Traoré's leadership is not limited to Burkina Faso; it serves as a catalyst for a larger Pan-African movement aimed at changing the continent's course.

The Ongoing Transformation And What Lies Ahead

Burkina Faso has embarked on a new course under Ibrahim Traoré's leadership, one characterized by independence, resiliency, and a rejection of outside domination. Although the change he started is still ongoing, its effects are already apparent in the government, economics, and security of the nation. How well his vision is maintained and extended will determine Burkina

Faso's and Africa's destiny as his administration continues to enact changes.

The total overhaul of Burkina Faso's military policy is among the biggest ongoing changes under Traoré's direction. He has concentrated on creating an independent military that isn't dependent on other forces for protection ever since he came to office. He has established a security system that puts national sovereignty first by bolstering local defense organizations, boosting military recruiting, and investing in cutting-edge weapons. Improved counterterrorism measures have already resulted from this change, since the nation has made significant progress in regaining areas that were previously under militant control.

In terms of the economy, Burkina Faso is moving toward independence. To guarantee that the nation retains the income from gold and other resources, Traoré's administration has taken decisive action to renegotiate mining contracts. The state is attempting to promote local companies, increase agricultural output, and lessen reliance on imports for food. Instead of benefiting foreign firms, these initiatives seek to establish a sustainable economy that benefits Burkinabé residents. If this economic revolution is successful, other African countries aiming for financial independence may use it as a model.

Burkina Faso's involvement in the Alliance of Sahel States (AES) is still developing at the regional level. Moving away from conventional Western-backed groups like ECOWAS, the nation is constructing a joint security and economic policy with Mali and Niger. If this coalition is successful, it might change the power dynamics in West Africa and provide a new framework for regional integration that puts African interests ahead of outside intervention.

But there are still difficulties. Traoré's agenda is at danger from internal opposition from political elites, possible isolation from global financial institutions, and the prospect of economic penalties from Western countries. While negotiating geopolitical demands from international forces that oppose his rejection of neocolonialism, his administration must figure out how to maintain economic development.

Traoré continues to have widespread public support, particularly among young people who see him as a leader dedicated to genuine change. Making sure his changes endure when he leaves office, however, will be the real measure of his leadership. His influence will last for centuries if he can establish a political system that fosters long-term national growth, institutionalize his ideas, and nurture future leaders who share his vision.

Burkina Faso has both possibilities and challenges in store for the future. The nation may become a major player in the emerging Pan-African movement if it can effectively handle the difficulties of economic independence, security stability, and diplomatic realignment. Although Traoré's leadership has brought about a change, the process is far from finished. Whether Burkina Faso can maintain this momentum and spur more extensive reform across Africa is the true test.

CONCLUSION

For Burkina Faso and the African continent as a whole, Ibrahim Traoré's leadership represents a sea change. By standing up to the forces of neocolonialism, economic exploitation, and foreign control that have long kept African states behind, his audacious efforts have challenged the current quo. He has quickly redefined what it means to lead with purpose, demonstrating that genuine change can be brought about by independence, solidarity, and steadfast dedication to the people.

Traoré has set the stage for a Burkina Faso free from foreign influence by emphasizing economic independence, regional collaboration, and national sovereignty. He has established a strong precedent by pushing for intra-African cooperation, renegotiating resource management, and rejecting outside military intervention. He has served as a reminder to Africa that independence must be earned, gained, and protected.

However, Traoré's influence goes beyond the boundaries of Burkina Faso. A new generation of leaders, activists, and people have been inspired to reconsider Africa's destiny by his leadership, which has rekindled the spirit of pan-Africanism. He has shown that independence is a decision and that it takes bravery, planning, and cooperation to overcome it. His partnership with Mali and Niger has shown that African countries are capable of resolving their own issues and creating new avenues for independence from outside influence.

However, there are obstacles along the way. His fortitude will be put to the test by international conflicts, internal resistance, and economic constraints. The long-term institutions and mechanisms he creates for next generations will be the real test of his success, not merely the improvements he makes now. Burkina Faso may become a symbol of self-determination and demonstrate that Africa can develop on its own terms if his vision is maintained.

More significantly, Africans are waking up as the rest of the world watches. Traoré has ignited a movement that transcends national boundaries and individual leaders. It is an exhortation to Africans to take back their destiny, unite against exploitation, and create a continent that prospers on its own resources, power, and solidarity. His leadership is a proclamation that Africa's future is the continent's own, not just a revolution.